300

Crazy Football Facts

For Football Fanatics

The FIFA World Cup is the most watched sports event in the world and it was estimated that World Cup 2018, which was played in Russia, had a combined viewership of 3.572 billion

Did you know that the 2018 FIFA World Cup Final which was played between France and Croatia had a combined global audience of 1.12 billion

A city in South Yorkshire, England is the proud home of the world's oldest Football Club. Sheffield Football Club or Sheffield F.C. The Football club was founded on the 24th of October 1857

Back in December of 1942, Stephan Stanis scored a staggering 16 goals for his side Racing Club de Lens, not a single person, since then, has managed to break this bizarre record

Argentinians are a goal-scoring machine, and Lionel Messi is the living proof of this. But what is an amazing football fact is that on the 26th of December 1998, one day after Christmas, Ricardo Olivera made history by scoring a goal in mere 2.8 seconds.

A crazy fact is that some asteroids have been named after certain football icons such as Arsene Wenger, Johan Cruyff, Josef Bican, Ferenc Puskas and Michael. These asteroids went by the names: Ballack 33179, Arsènewenger14282, Cruyff10634, Pepibican82656 and Puskas79647

There is an official football club with the most letters. The Dutch football club which is often called NAC Breda. The full name of this Football Club from the Netherlands consists of 83 letters, yes! 83 letters.

NAC Breda stands for, Nooit Opgeven Altijd Doorzetten Aangenaam Door Vermaak En Nuttig Door Ontspanning Combinatie Breda.

The great Brazilian footballer Ronaldinho went on to become one of the best players the game of football has ever seen in the history of its existence. At the age of 13 years, the Brazilian footballer was part of a game where his local team won the game 23-0.

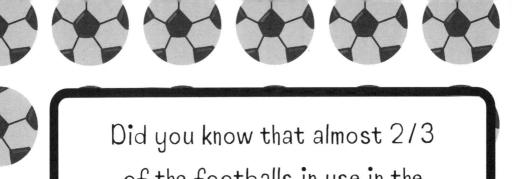

Did you know that almost 2/3 of the footballs in use in the World comes from Pakistan?

On average, a footballer (with obvious exception to the goalkeeper) covers a distance of 7 miles (11.2 kms)

We already know that Football is played by a huge population of the world, but did you know that a total of 210 countries are registered with FIFA and play the sport competitively making it the worlds most popular sport.

a total of 21 World Cup Torumenats have been hosted and in those 21 tournaments only 8 teams have won the Football World Cup Title. Brazil have the most wins with 5 world cup victories.

The very first game of Basketball played on the 21st of December 1891 was played using a football

In the 90 years of the FIFA World Cup, European countries have made it to every final with exception of two World Cup Finals.

Do you know that only 2 countries in the world call Football, Soccer? The two countries are America and Canada.

The very first official, international, match of football, as recognised by FIFA, was played on the 30th of November 1872 between England and Scotland. The match was attended by 4,000 people and resulted in a draw with the final score of 0-0.

In the 90s when there was less money and players had to do whatever it took to keep the game running, Mark Hughes, a Manchester United player and a Welsh star had to feature in two football matches in a single day.

It was England who came up with the word Soccer but stopped using the word more than 35 years ago.

The biggest football and sports stadium in the world is located in North Korea. It is known as the Rungrado located in Pyongyang and has a capacity of 114,000!

The highest scoring game ever occurred on 31st October 2002 which saw a game of two arch-rivals A S Adema and SO L'Emyrne. SO L'Emyrne scored 149 own goals in protest to an unfair refereeing decision which lead to a final result of 149-0.

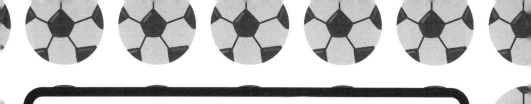

Argentinian star footballer Angel Di Maria, was once traded between two of his homeland football clubs for 35 footballs

---

Kazuyoshi Miura of Japan is a 53 year old footballer who plays for Yokohama FC in the Forward position. He is the oldest professional to have played.

There is still one country who has remained undefeated facing Brazil. Norway have played 4 matches against Brazil and came out victorious twice and two times the matched ended up in a draw.

Neymar holds the record for the most expensive transfer fee when he was bought by Paris Saint-Germain from Barcelona for £198 million

Rogerio Ceni, A Brazilian footballer has scored 131 goals as a goal keeper from 1200 games for Sao Paulo FC

Kazuyoshi Miura of Japan is a 53 year old footballer who plays for Yokohama FC in the Forward position. He is the oldest professional to have played.

The Longest unbeaten steak recorded is held by Steaua Bucharest, a Romanian football club went 106 matches unbeaten and through this huge feat won 5 straight league titles along with the 1985-86 European Cup.

The size of a football has remained exactly the same for 120 years. It still has the same circumference of 28 inches.

A game in 5th tier Argentinean football between arch rivals Claypole and Victoriano Arenas saw 36 Red Cards when all hell broke loose between players and benches.

An amazing football fact is that the word FIFA stands for Fédération Internationale de Football Association which is French for International Federation of Football Association.

The year was 2005 and the competition was Namibian Cup when KK Palace and Civics were facing each other and it took a total of record breaking 48 spots kicks to settle the match making it the longest penalty shootout ever.

In the year 1937, British Broadcast Corporation (BBC) the first ever live football match. It was a match played between Arsenal and Arsenal Reserves.

Did you know that Pele was just 11 when he was discovered by the scouts and by the age of 16 he had already started playing professional football. If this is interesting, here is a bonus football fact for you that at the age of 17 he played his first FIFA World Cup (1958) and scored 6 goals helping Brazil win their first World Cup.

Miroslav Klose, the German footballer hold the record of scoring most number of goals in World Cups. He has scored 16 in total which is 1 more than Brazilian star Ronaldo.

The year was 2005 and the competition was Namibian Cup when KK Palace and Civics were facing each other and it took a total of record breaking 48 spots kicks to settle the match making it the longest penalty shootout ever.

Every player used to wear the same jersey including the goalkeeper from a team until 1909 when goalkeepers were asked to wear a different colour from the teams jersey.

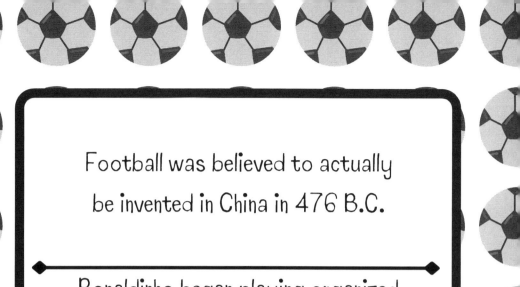

Football was believed to actually be invented in China in 476 B.C.

Ronaldinho began playing organized youth soccer at the age of 7, and it was as a youth football player that he first received the nickname "Ronaldinho".

Pele was the first to call football "the beautiful game".

The total length of the football field is 100 yards.

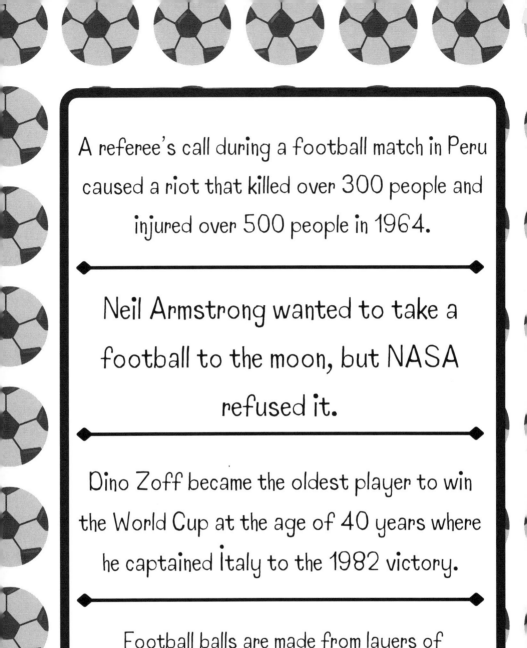

A referee's call during a football match in Peru caused a riot that killed over 300 people and injured over 500 people in 1964.

Neil Armstrong wanted to take a football to the moon, but NASA refused it.

Dino Zoff became the oldest player to win the World Cup at the age of 40 years where he captained Italy to the 1982 victory.

Football balls are made from layers of synthetic leather while the bladders inside the ball are made from latex or butyl.

Lee Todd holds the record of receiving the fastest red card in the history of professional football after he used foul language.

FIFA has more member countries in it than the U.N.

One of the largest ever football tournaments took place in the year 1999 in which a total of 5,098 teams had participated. It was for the second Bangkok League Seven-a-Side competition in which more than 35,000 players took part.

The highest number of goals ever scored by one player in a single football match was 16 in the year 1942 in December. It was scored by a player named Stephan Stanis from France who was playing for a club known as Racing Club de Lens.

On an average, a football player runs for an average of 9.65 km during each game, which is the equivalent of about 15 km.

FIFA has more member countries in it than the U.N.

One of the largest ever football tournaments took place in the year 1999 in which a total of 5,098 teams had participated. It was for the second Bangkok League Seven-a-Side competition in which more than 35,000 players took part.

As per the evidence recorded on video footage, one of the fastest ever goal was scored by a player named Ricardo Olivera from Uruguay in the month of December in the year 1998. He scored the goal in a total of 2.8 seconds.

On an average, more than one in 20 injuries that happen during a football match are a result of the celebration of scoring a goal on the pitch.

The highest number of goals scored in a Football World Cup match was in the year 1982 when Hungary scored ten goals against El Salvador.

The only footballer who ever scored a winning goal for San Marino was Andy Selva. He scored their only winning goal in the year 2004 against Liechtenstein to score a 1-0 victory. Out of the total 121 games that San Marino played, the team had a record win of 1 game, three draws, and 117 losses.

Footballer Andy Selva also holds the distinction of being his nation's all-time top goal scorer. He had scored 8 goals out of the 64 appearances he made.

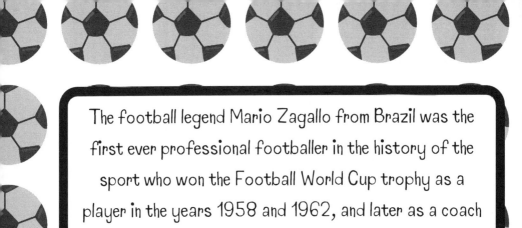

The football legend Mario Zagallo from Brazil was the first ever professional footballer in the history of the sport who won the Football World Cup trophy as a player in the years 1958 and 1962, and later as a coach in the year 1970.

Did you know that Gordon Ramsey, who is today known the world over as a celebrity chef had been scouted by Rangers but had to leave his dream of becoming a professional footballer after he suffered a knee injury.

Out of the 12 host cities for the 2014 FIFA World Cup in Brazil, 8 are considered to be among the 50 most violent cities around the world.

Mesut Ozil is a German football player who donated his World Cup victory bonus pay of 300,000 euro to help pay for the surgeries of 23 children in Brazil.

In the year 1967, the two sides that were involved in the Nigerian Civil War decided to go on a ceasefire for 48 hours, so that they could watch football player Pele play in an exhibition match in Lagos.

In the year 1998, a bolt of lightning struck a football match field in Congo. An entire football team was wiped off as all 11 members of the same team died whereas the members of the other team were not touched by the lightning strike. The match was being played between the villages of nearby Basangana and BenaTshadi.

In the year 2011, it cost more than 30 million US dollars to advertise a 30 second commercial during the Super Bowl. During the Football World Cup matches, more than one billion fans watch the game on television.

Greenland is not able to join the FIFA because not enough grass grows there for a football field.

Chelsea are the only team to be holders of the Europa League and the Champions League at the same time. In 2012, the Blues won their first Champions League. The following season, with Rafa Benitez at the helm, the club won the Europa League final, on 15 May. Given that the Champions League final was due on May 25, for 10 days only, Chelsea were the holders of both titles.

Nemanja Vidic is the only Premier League winner with a surname made entirely of Roman Numerals. V is five, I is one, D is 500 and C is 100.

Portsmouth hold the record for having held the FA Cup for the longest – seven years – despite only winning it once in that time. This was because they won it in 1939 and there was no professional football during the war.

Bixente Lizarazu was the first World and European Champion at both club and international level. The Frenchman won the Champions League final and Intercontinental Cup in 2001 with Bayern Munich, after lifting the World Cup in 1998 and the European Championship in 2000.

New Zealand were the only unbeaten team in the 2010 World Cup. New Zealand's three draws weren't enough to see them out of their group.

The first Englishman to manage at a World Cup final was not Alf Ramsey, but George Raynor. Raynor did it eight years earlier with Sweden.

Only one team have ever won the World Cup final playing in red. England.

Fernando Torres was captain of the Atletico Madrid side that Diego Simeone played in.

Dundee United have a 100% record against Barcelona. Played four, won four.

In 2014, three Chelsea goalkeepers were awarded clean sheets in a 0-0 draw with Atletico Madrid. Mark Schwarzer came off the bench to replace Petr Cech in the 18th minute with the score goalless. Schwarzer didn't concede and neither did the Atletico keeper, Thibault Courtois... who was on loan from Chelsea.

David Beckham and David Moyes used to play together. Moyes was at Preston North End from 1993 to 1999 – while Beckham played the 1994/95 season at Deepdale on loan from Manchester United.

Robert Earnshaw is the only player to have scored a hat-trick in all three divisions of the English Football League, the Premier League, the League Cup, FA Cup, and for his country at International level.

Javier Mascherano's first game in senior football was for Argentina's national team, not for his club at the time, River Plate.

Chelsea legend Gianfranco Zola is the only player to be sent off in a World Cup finals... on his birthday.

The 1968 European Championship semi-final was decided by a coin toss. Italy beat the Soviet Union on the toss and later won in the final.

The highest attendance recorded at Old Trafford was 76,962 for an FA Cup semi-final between Wolverhampton Wanderers and Grimsby Town on 25 March 1939.

The last time both European Cup/Champions League finalists had no foreign players in their starting XIs was in 1967.

While she was a director at Birmingham City Karren Brady sold her husband Paul Peschisolido to Stoke for £400k

Ferenc Puskas, the greatest Hungarian footballer ever, played for Spain at the 1962 World Cup

In 1975, the Manchester United goalkeeper, Alex Stepney dislocated his jaw while shouting at his defenders

Since 1982 at least one Bayern Munich player has played in every World Cup final.

Feyenoord goalkeeper Ronald Graafland waited 18 years to make his senior league debut for the club after first joining them

---

Before Alex Ferguson took over at Manchester United, Aston Villa were the more successful club.

Peter Osgood's ashes are buried under the penalty spot at the Shed End of Stamford Bridge

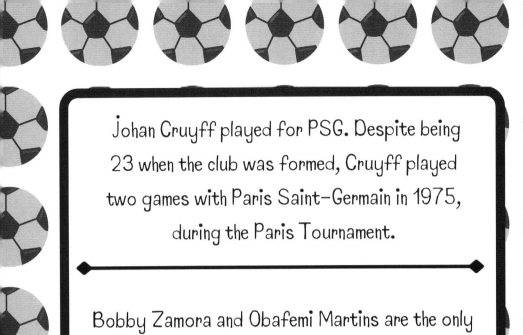

Johan Cruyff played for PSG. Despite being 23 when the club was formed, Cruyff played two games with Paris Saint-Germain in 1975, during the Paris Tournament.

Bobby Zamora and Obafemi Martins are the only two footballers to have scored penalties with their right and left foot in the Premier League.

Only one of Ruud Van Nistelrooy's 150 goals for Manchester United was from outside the box.

France were awarded the first penalty by VAR at the 2018 World Cup, in a group game against Australia

St Johnstone is the only team in Britain with a J in it.

Only three times has the world transfer record been broken by teams not from Italy, England or Spain. Paris Saint-Germain most recently broke it for Neymar with the other two teams being River Plate and Falkirk. In 1932, River paid £32,000 for Bernabé Ferreyra; 10 years prior, Falkirk paid £5,000 for West Ham United's Sydney Puddlefoot.

The U.S. Men won both silver and bronze at the 1904 Olympics.

Widzew Lodz is the only club this century to defend the title of second division champions. They won it in 2007/08 and got promoted to Ekstraklasa but were relegated back down immediately, due to their involvement in a corruption scandal. In 2008/09, they won it again.

The only player to have won European Cup winners' medals with two different English clubs is Jimmy Rimmer.

Only three times has the world transfer record been broken by teams not from Italy, England or Spain. Paris Saint-Germain most recently broke it for Neymar with the other two teams being River Plate and Falkirk. In 1932, River paid £32,000 for Bernabé Ferreyra; 10 years prior, Falkirk paid £5,000 for West Ham United's Sydney Puddlefoot.

The first World Cup hat trick and clean sheet were by Americans. Them again. United States goalkeeper Jimmy Douglas managed the first clean sheet of the inaugural 1930 tournament in a 3–0 win against Belgium.

In 2003 Club President Franz Beckenbauer threatened the German league with moving Bayern Munich to Italy.

Bringing celery to Stamford Bridge is outlawed and could get you a lifetime ban.

Coventry City did not finish in the top six of any division between 1970 and 2018.

The Arsenal captain always chooses the length of the entire team's sleeves for the game.

AC and İnter Milan were one club who split due to a dispute.

Owen Hargreaves is the only player to have played for England without having previously lived in the United Kingdom.

Coventry City did not finish in the top six of any division between 1970 and 2018.

Arsenal and Port Vale are the only two clubs in the country that don't have the geographical location of the team in their name.

Gareth Bale's first trophyless season after leaving Tottenham was the season he went back to Tottenham.

The Brunei national team used to enter Malaysian club competitions and won the Malaysian Cup in 1999.

Samuel Eto'o won consecutive trebles in 2009 and 2010 with Barcelona and Inter Milan.

Luka Modric and Mark Viduka are cousins.

10 of France's top 12 most-capped players played in the Euro 2000 final.

Patrick Kluivert and Ruud van Nistelrooy were born on the exact same day.

In 1996, Eidur Gudjohnsen was subbed on for Arnor Gudjohnsen, making them the first (and still only) father and son to appear in the same international match.

Goalkeeper Hans-Jorg Butt scored three Champions League goals – all penalties for different clubs against Juventus.

France went 20 years from 1986 vs Belgium in Mexico to not winning a World Cup game on foreign soil.

Steve Finnan is the only player to have played in the World Cup, Champions League, UEFA Cup, and the top 5 levels of English football.

Neither Manchester United nor Liverpool have ever beaten Gillingham in a competitive match.

John Obi Mikel's actual name is Michael: Mikel was a spelling error

West Ham defender Alvin Martin's first ever hat trick was scored against three different Newcastle goalkeepers.

Mario Balotelli's only Premier League assist ever was for Sergio Aguero's dramatic title-winning goal in 2011/12.

John Terry scored more Premier League goals for Chelsea than Andres Iniesta scored La Liga goals for Barcelona.

In the 1930 World Cup, 300 people attended a match between Romania and Peru. One week later 80,000 attended the Uruguay v Romania match

Three England captains have played for Scunthorpe United. Kevin Keegan, Ray Clemence and Sir Ian Botham.

Boca Juniors got their kit colours from Sweden. In 1906, Boca Juniors played Nottingham de Almagro. Both teams wore similar black and white kits, so played a game to decide who would keep the colours. Boca lost, and decided to adopt the colours of the flag of the first boat to sail into the port at La Boca. This turned out to be a Swedish ship resulting in a blue and yellow kit.

When Groningen were promoted in 1971 they had only conceded seven goals during the entire season. All seven goals were scored in seven different matches, yet Groningen didn't even win the league, coming second that year.

Ryan Giggs was never sent off for Manchester United with 963 appearances.

Queen's Park, a team from Glasgow, have played in two FA Cup finals.

Every player who played in Shinji Kagawa's first international game for Japan against Ivory Coast in 2008, was still playing professional football 10 years later.

The first 50 Premier League goals scored by Bosnians all came from Edin Dzeko. The 51st came from Asmir Begovic.

The first two players born in a re-unified Germany combined for the World Cup-winning goal. Mario Gotze and Andre Schurrle.

Alfredo Di Stefano was offered on loan to Manchester United, but the move was blocked by the FA.

Libya have played in the opening game in every African Cup of Nations that they have participated in.

Paolo Maldini captained AC Milan to a Champions League final win in England exactly 40 years after his father did the same.

Dejan Stankovic has played for three different national teams at World Cups. The former Inter Milan man represented Yugoslavia at their last tournament in 1998, before playing for Serbia and Montenegro in 2006 and an independent Serbia side in 2010.

There are only two players who have played in three European Cup finals for three different clubs. Clarence Seedorf won the tournament with Ajax in 1995, Real Madrid in 2000 and AC Milan in 2003 and 2007 – but Patrice Evra was not so lucky.

In the 1950 World Cup, England were beaten 1-0 by the USA – and the goalscorer wasn't even a US citizen.

AC Milan won the 1993/94 Serie A by only scoring 36 goals.

Thomas Muller has never scored in the European Championship.

Ryan Giggs has been substituted more times than any other player (134).

Wayne Rooney, Gareth Bale and Kevin Davies are the only players to score, assist and score an own goal in a single Premier League game.

Man United have never lost a Premier League game at Old Trafford in which they have been ahead at half-time.

Alan Shearer has missed the most Premier League penalties (11). He's also scored the most (56).

2015/16 was the first time West Ham had recorded a positive goal difference in a top-flight season since 1985/86.

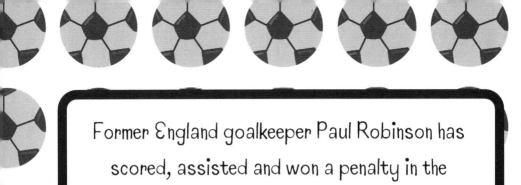

Former England goalkeeper Paul Robinson has scored, assisted and won a penalty in the Premier League. He also has more Premier League assists than any other keeper (five).

James Milner has scored in 47 different Premier League games – and hasn't lost any of them (a record).

The only person born before 1960 to score a Premier League hat-trick is Gordan Strachan.

In 2014/15, George Boyd became the fourth player to play for two relegated teams in the same Premier League campaign (others were Mark Robins in 94/95, Steve Kabba in 06/07 and David Nugent in 09/10).

In 2014/15, Leicester City spent longer at the bottom of the table without being relegated than any side in Premier League history (140 days).

Cesar Azpilicueta (2016/17), Wes Morgan (2015/16), John Terry (2014/15) and Gary Pallister (1992/93) are the only outfield players to play every minute of the season for a Premier League title-winning side.

Peter Crouch has scored more headed goals (50) than 16 of the teams who have played in the Premier League.

Nuri Sahin (formerly at Liverpool) has played the most Premier League games of any player to be substituted off in all of their PL appearances (7).

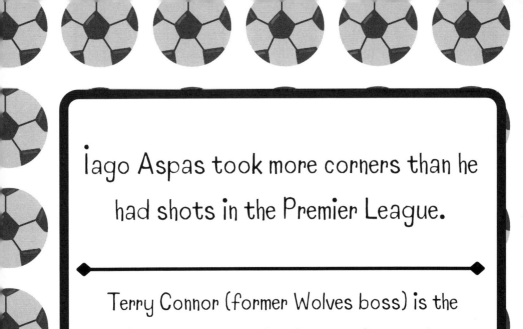

Iago Aspas took more corners than he had shots in the Premier League.

Terry Connor (former Wolves boss) is the only manager to take charge of more than 10 Premier League games and not win a single one.

In 2016/17, Hull became only the third team to be top of the Premier League and be relegated in the same season (after Charlton in 1998/99 and Bolton in 2011/12).

Only two players have ever scored a hat-trick of headers in a Premier League match: Duncan Ferguson for Everton (vs Bolton in December 1997) and Salomon Rondon for West Brom (vs Swansea in December 2016).

The first British football club to reach a European Champions Cup Semi Final was Hibernian of Scotland in season 1955-56.

Harry Redknapp is the only manager to win the Premier League Manager of the Month Award for four different clubs.

The Soviet Union (USSR) won the first European Football Championships in 1960.

The first time player\s shirt numbers were used was on 25th August 1928 when Sheffield Wednesday beat Arsenal 3-2. Wednesday wore numbers 1 to 11 while Arsenal wore numbers 12 to 22.

The first British player to be transferred for £110,000 was Denis Law from Manchester City to Torino (Italy) in June 1961.

Coventry City, Newcastle United and Oldham Athletic. were originally called Singers FC, Stanley AFC and Pine Villa FC

The only FIFA World Cup tournament not to have a Final match was in Brazil 1950. The top four teams (Brazil, Spain, Sweden & Uruguay) played in a mini-league against each other. Uruguay finished champions.

The first club to win the European — South American Intercontinental Cup in 1960 was Real Madrid of Spain when they beat Peñarol of Uruguay over two legs. The competition ran until 2004, when it was replaced with FIFA's Club World Cup.

The only manager to win the FIFA World Cup twice (till 2018) was Vittorio Pozzo of Italy in 1934 & 1938.

The first two brothers who played against each other in a FIFA World Cup Finals tournament was during the 2010 Finals in South Africa when Jerome Boateng's Germany beat Kevin-Prince Boateng's Ghana 1-0.

The two Nations that won the most Olympic Games Men's Football gold medals (till 2016) at 3 each are Hungary in 1952, 1964 & 1968 and Great Britain in 1900, 1908 & 1912.

The first league was created in 1888, in England.

Richard Dunne has scored the most EPL own goals with a total of 10.

Cristiano Ronaldo is the most followed person on Instagram with 423 million followers and counting!

The record in the EPL Shane Long was clocked at 21.94 mph. Usain Bolt record on a track is 27.8 mph.

Thomas Langu Sweswe, a Zimbabwe player, played for 90 minutes and didn't touch the ball.

Zinedine Zidane was never offside in his entire career.

Celtic beat Barcelona 2-1 with 11% ball possession.

Willian has more champions league goals than Ronaldinho.

It took Ronaldo 30 games before he scored his first Champions League goal. He is now the all time leading goal scorer in the competition.

Philipp Lahm once went 13 months without committing a foul.

Benjamin Aguero is the son of Sergio Aguero, Grandchild of Diego Maradona and Messi is his God-father.

Kingsley Coman has won the League every season of his professional career (PSG, Juventus, and Bayern)

Wayne Rooney, Gareth Bale, and Kevin Davies are the only players to score, assist and score an own goal in a single Premier League game.

Spain Won the 2010 World Cup with only 8 eight goals throughout the competition.

Marcelo has never played in the Copa America.

Gary Lineker never received a yellow card in his career.

Giroud's scorpion kick goal won the Puskas award but didn't win goal of the month.

Benteke has more Premier League goals than Eric Cantona.

Real Madrid beat their own reserve side in the 1980 Copa Del Rey final.

Zlatan İbrahimovic has played for six clubs that have won the Champions League, but he has never actually won the trophy himself.

Chelsea have been relegated as many times as they have won the league (6).

Theo Walcott has more Champions League goals than Brazilian Ronaldo, Hazard, David Villa, Klose, Zidane, Huntelaar, Tevez, Alexis Sanchez, and Michael Owen.

Jose Mourinho went nine years without losing a home game.

Juan Mata is the first player in history to have joined Manchester United from Chelsea

Steven Gerrard has swapped his jersey with more than a hundred players, but never with a Man United player.

Stefan Schwarz had a bizarre "Space clause" in his Sunderland contract.

Steve Bruce once scored 19 goals from centre-back in a season.

Jose Mourinho didn't win a single Manager of the Month award in two of his three Premier League title winning seasons.

Wolfsburg once had a manager named Wolfgang Wolf.

Sergio Ramos has played with both Zinedine Zidane and Zidane's son at Real Madrid.

Alex Song has 27 siblings — 17 sisters and 10 brothers.

Ex Liverpool keeper Simon Mignolet speaks 5 languages and has a degree in politics.

Dundee United have played and beaten Barcelona 4 times in professional fixtures, giving them a 100% win record.

Ronaldo (the Brazilian) has never won the Champions League despite playing for 5 teams that did.

Manuel Neuer stars in the German version of the 2013 Disney/Pixar film 'Monsters University'. He provides the voice for the character Frank McCay.

Former Liverpool man Charlie Adam is younger than Cristiano Ronaldo.

The first English team to win a European trophy is West Auckland Town FC. They won the Sir Thomas Lipton trophy, one of football's first European competitions, twice in 1909 and 1911.

The FIFA World Cup is the most-watched sporting event in the world.

The first World Cup was held in 1930 in Uruguay; 13 teams competed and Uruguay won.

Soccer is the most lucrative sport in the world. The soccer industry produces more money than any other sport.

Singapore's national football stadium is a giant floating field anchored in Marina Bay.

A 2000 internet poll voted Argentine Diego Maradona "the player of the century." FIFA disagreed strongly enough that they appointed a special committee to render judgment. The committee selected Pelé.

Brazilians refer to soccer as the "jogo bonito" or "beautiful game."

A medical survey found that professional soccer players sustained approximately 1.5 injuries per player per year.

Part of soccer's worldwide popularity can be attributed to colonialism; the British took the game with them in their exploration and colonization of the world.

The second World Cup was hosted in Italy. Because Italy had refused to attend the World Cup hosted by Uruguay, Uruguay chose to snub Italy, making the second cup the only time a champion team was not present to defend their title.

Andre Villas-Boas made £11 million-a-year coaching Shanghai SIPG in the CSL.

Costa Rica never lost a match in regular or extra time at the 2014 World Cup. They were eliminated in the quarterfinals by the Netherlands in a penalty shoot-out.

Brazil had more shots (18-14), shots on target (13-12) and possession (52-48) than Germany in their 1-7 defeat in the semifinals of the 2014 World Cup.

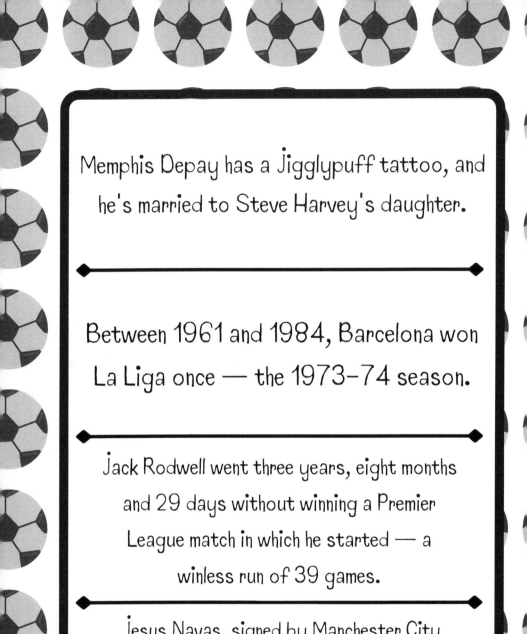

Memphis Depay has a Jigglypuff tattoo, and he's married to Steve Harvey's daughter.

Between 1961 and 1984, Barcelona won La Liga once — the 1973-74 season.

Jack Rodwell went three years, eight months and 29 days without winning a Premier League match in which he started — a winless run of 39 games.

Jesus Navas, signed by Manchester City for £14.9 million in 2013, ended his City career without a goal in more than 103 hours of EPL football — 115 matches.

Three teams have never been relegated from the Spanish Primera Division: Real Madrid, FC Barcelona and Athletic Bilbao.

In the 2007–08 season of the PL, Derby County managed just one win in the entire season. They ended the season with just 11 points.

Manchester City are the only side to pick up 100 EPL points in a season.

The youngest person to play in the Premier League is Harvey Elliot. He had just turned 16 (one month before) he played his debut alongside seasoned players for Wolverhampton Wanderers in 2019.

Real Madrid has won the most Champions League/ European Cup wins with 13.

There are many high-value players in the premier league but Mbappé has a transfer value of $423 million. He currently plays for Paris Saint-Germain.

Former Colombian international defender Gerardo Bedoya holds the world record for most red cards in a career with 41.

Former Fiorentina striker Adrian Mutu was banned for playing for Romania in 2013 after posting an image on Facebook comparing national team boss Victor Pițurcă to Mr. Bean.

Danish international Allan Nielsen was once side lined with an injury while playing for Tottenham Hotspur after his new born daughter poked him in the eye.

During World War I, English and German soldiers engaged in a "Christmas truce," and, appropriately enough given their storied rivalry on the pitch, played a friendly game of football.

The fastest hat trick of all time was scored in 90 seconds by Tommy Ross of Ross County, in November 1964.

Yossi Benayoun is the only player to have scored a hat trick in the Premier League, Champions League and FA Cup.

The only Bundesliga club to have never been relegated from the top flight since the league's formation is Bayern Munich.

While Zlatan Ibrahimovich's youth team was 4-0 down, he came in as a substitute and scored 8 goals.

Ryan Giggs is the only Premier League player to score 100 goals without scoring a hat- trick.

Brazilian legend, Pele, scored 92 hat-tricks, 4 goals on 31 occasions, 5 goals on 6 occasions, and 8 goals on an occasion.

Louis Van Gaal and David Moyes attended the same Tactical Management School.

Asmir Begovich scored from 97.5 yards for Stoke City Vs Southampton.

Lionel Messi scored 91 goals in 2012 making it the highest top flight goals in a calendar year.

Referees were not used in official soccer matches until 1881.

Oleg Salenko of Russia holds the record for most goals scored in a single World Cup match. He was able to score 5 in Russia's win over Cameron.

Mexico City and Rio de Janeiro are the only two places to host a World Cup final multiple times.

The United States has dominated the Women's World Cup since the inaugural 1991 tournament. They have four titles and one runner up out of the eight tournaments.

Did you know that until 1991, soccer was an illegal sport in Mississippi?

The national sport of Canada is soccer.

Brazil have the most world cup goals with 229 in total.

The first international match played outside the British Isles was between Uruguay and Argentina in 1902.

Neymar won the La Liga player of the month award before Lionel Messi did.

The first black professional football player was Arthur Wharton. He was born in the Gold Coast, now Ghana. He was Rotherham United's goalkeeper way back in 1889.

In the football World Cup, the most common score is 1—0, whereas in the English top division it is 1–1.

In the early days of football there were no fouls, it was a game played by gentlemen and so all that was needed was an apology if there was any ungentlemanly behaviour.

The smallest attendance at a Football World Cup finals match was just 300. The infamous match was between Romania and Peru during the 1930 World Cup in Uruguay.

The penalty spot in football was invented as a time and cost saving measure in the late 1800s. Originally, the penalty line was drawn completely across the whole pitch.

Edin Dzeko scored the first goal to be awarded by goal-line technology in 2014.

Kylian Mbappe became the youngest player to score in a World Cup final since Pele in 2018.

Only two players have scored a hat trick of headers in the Premier League. Duncan Ferguson for Everton Vs Bolton in 1997 and Salomon Rondon for West Bromwich Albion Vs Swansea in 2016.

Dennis Bergkamp is the only player to win the 1st, 2nd and 3rd prizes for goal of the month.

Arsenal's 'invincibles' are the only team to have received a golden Premier League trophy.

The game initially had around 15 players per team, later reduced to 11 in 1880.

Women started playing soccer around the same time as men did in England. However, originally men were the main players in the game. Women's soccer started to become a lot more popular in the 1990s.

In 2020, Spain's
Euro's squad including
no Real Madrid players.

The last time Karim Benzema played in
an international tournament for France,
Barack Obama was still US president.

Argentina have won the world cup twice
and there was only one player who played
in both named Daniel Passarella.

Cristiano Ronaldo had scored
more international goals than 18
teams at Euro 2020.

Ronald Koeman is the top scoring defender of all time.

No players from Germany's squad in the 2020 Euro's had ever scored a goal at a European Championship.

Antonin Panenka scored the winning penalty in a game Vs Germany in the 1976 Euro's final where he chipped the goalkeeper to have the iconic penalty named after him.

Only 4 European players have won more than one world cup and they all played for Italy in 1934 and 1938.

Fernando Torres is the only player to have scored in 7 competitions in the same football season.

The Amount of Bets per Game in the 2018 World Cup was €2.1 Billion.

The First English Team to Reach European Cup Finals Is Birmingham City.

Bolivia Defeated Argentina 6-1 in A Game That Involved Lionel Messi In 2009.

Fernando Torres is the only player to have scored in 7 competitions in the same football season.

The Amount of Bets per Game in the 2018 World Cup was €2.1 Billion.

The First English Team to Reach a European Cup Finals Is Birmingham City.

Bolivia Defeated Argentina 6-1 in A Game That Involved Lionel Messi In 2009.

Denmark won the 1992 Euros after not even initially qualifying.

Chris Nicholl scored all four goals in a 2—2 draw between Aston Villa and Leicester City on 20 March 1976.

There have been more red cards shown in games between Liverpool and Everton than in any other fixture in Premier League History.

Manchester United won 25 points away from home in 2010—11; the fewest away points by a Premier League champion in a season.

Sir Alex Ferguson has recorded 30 victories against Everton in the Premier League — a competition high for a manager beating a specific team.

Sir Stanley Mathews was the oldest players to play in the English first division at 50 years old and for England at 42 years old.

Sir Stanley Mathews was the first Ballon d'Or winner in 1956.

Lionel Messi has the most Ballon d'Or awards with 7 awards.

Lev Yashin is the only goalkeeper to have ever won the Ballon d'or in 1963.

Ac Milan signed Andrea Pirlo from arch rivals İnter Milan.

George Weah was the first non European and first African player to win the Ballon d'Or in 1995.

Ballon d'Or translates to 'Golden Ball' in English.

Ian Wright made his premier league debut at 28 years old.

Lusail, the city that will host the 2022 FIFA World Cup final game does not yet exist.

Erling Haaland was born in Leeds, England.

The sport is played in over 200 countries by 250 million players.

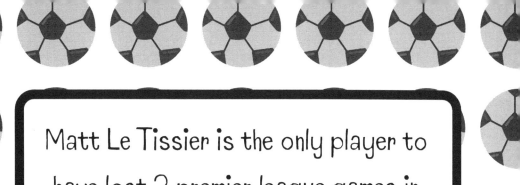

Matt Le Tissier is the only player to have lost 2 premier league games in which he scored a hat trick.

The last all English 11 players and first all foreign 11 players took place in 1999. Aston Villa and Chelsea respectively.

The last time neither Celtic or Rangers didn't win the first Scottish division league was in the 1984/85 season to Aberdeen managed by Sir Alex Ferguson.

A club receives £100k for winning the English football league cup.

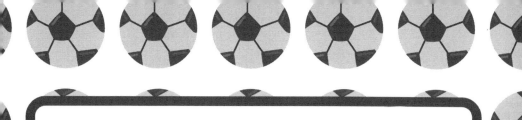

Scan The QR Code To Check Out More Utopia Press Books On Amazon!

Printed in Great Britain
by Amazon

10565729R00045